EVERYTHING ABORTION

All You Need To Know About Abortion

By

JANET BAYER

TABLE OF CONTENTS

INTRODUCTION

Abortion is the termination of a pregnancy by evacuation or ejection of an embryo or fetus. An abortion that happens without mediation is known as a miscarriage or "spontaneous Abortion "; these happen in roughly 30% to 40% of pregnancies. At the point when intentional actions are taken to end a pregnancy, it is called an induced abortion, or less commonly "induced miscarriage ". The unmodified word abortion, by and large, refers to an induced abortion. When an abortion is properly done, induced abortion is perhaps the most secure medical procedure. In the US, the risk of maternal mortality is multiple times lower after induced abortion than after labor. Nonetheless, hazardous abortions — those performed by individuals coming up short on the important and necessary skills, or in deficiently resourced settings — are a significant reason for maternal mortality, particularly in a developing country. Research shows that if abortion is made legal, safe, and accessible it reduces maternal mortality.

Medical or surgical procedures are the modern way of performing an abortion. The medication mifepristone in blend with prostaglandin gives off an impression of being just about as protected and viable as a medical procedure during the first and second trimester of pregnancy. The most well-known surgical procedure involves dilating the cervix and utilizing a pull gadget (a suction device). Contraceptives, like the pill or intrauterine gadgets, can be utilized quickly following abortion. When performed lawfully and securely on a lady who wants it, induced abortion doesn't expand the risk of long-haul mental or actual issues. Conversely, risky abortions (those performed by untalented people, with unsafe hardware, or in unsanitary offices) cause 47,000 deaths and 5 million emergency clinic admission every year.

Around 56 million abortions are done every year in the world, with around 45% done dangerously. Abortion rates changed little somewhere in the range of 2003 and 2008, preceding which they diminished for no less than twenty years as admittance to family arranging and conception prevention expanded. Starting around 2018, 37% of the world's women approached legitimate abortion unbounded as to reason. Nations that grant abortion have various cutoff points on how late in pregnancy abortion is permitted. abortion rates are comparative between nations that place a ban on Abortion and nations that permit it.

Historically, abortions have been done using herbal prescriptions, sharp devices, strong massage, or other customary strategies. Abortion regulations and social or strict perspectives on abortion are different all over the world. In certain areas, abortion is legitimate just in unambiguous cases like assault, fetal imperfections, poverty, risk to maternal health, or incest. There is banter over the moral, ethical, and lawful issues of abortion. The people who go against Abortion frequently contend that a fetus or embryo is an individual with a right to life, and subsequently liken abortion to murder. The people who support the lawfulness of abortion frequently contend that it is important for a lady's all in all correct to come to conclusions about her own body. Others favor legitimate and open abortion as a general well-being measure.

CHAPTER ONE

ABORTION: MEANING

Abortion is the removal of a fetus from the uterus before it has arrived at the phase of viability (in humans, ordinarily about the twentieth week of growth). Abortion might happen immediately, in which case it is called a miscarriage, or it could be done deliberately, in which case it is called an induced abortion. Miscarriages happen for some reasons, including illness, injury, hereditary deformity, or biochemical incompatibility of mother and baby. At times a fetus's death occur in the uterus yet it is not expelled out, a condition named a missed abortion.

Induced Abortions might be performed because of reasons that fall into four general classifications: to save the life or physical or mental health of the mother; to forestall the fruition of a pregnancy that has come about because of assault or incest; to forestall the birth of a kid with serious distortion, mental inadequacy, or hereditary irregularity; or to forestall a birth for social or monetary reasons. By certain definitions, abortions that are performed to save the health of the female or in instances of assault or incest are therapeutic or justifiable.

Various clinical procedures exist for performing Abortions. During the first trimester (up to around 12 weeks after conception), endometrial aspiration, suction, or curettage might be utilized to eliminate the fetus in the uterus. In endometrial aspiration, a thin and flexible tube is embedded up the cervical channel and afterward sucks out the lining of the uterus (the endometrium) through an electric siphon.

In the related yet somewhat more burdensome procedure known as dilatation and evacuation (likewise called suction curettage, or vacuum curettage), the cervical channel is broadened by the inclusion of a progression of metal dilators while the patient is under sedation, after which an unbending suction tube is embedded into the uterus to empty its contents. Instead of suction, a slight metal instrument called a curette is utilized to scratch (as opposed to vacuum out) the items in the uterus, the technique is called dilatation and curettage. When joined with dilatation, both evacuation and curettage can be utilized till about the sixteenth week of pregnancy.

From 12 to 19 weeks the infusion of a saline arrangement might be utilized to set off uterine contractions; then again, the use of prostaglandins by infusion, suppository, or other technique might be utilized to instigate contractions, but these substances might cause extreme side effects. Hysterotomy, the careful evacuation of the uterine content, might be utilized during the second trimester or later. As a general rule, the further developed the pregnancy, the more prominent the risk of maternal mortality or serious complexities following an abortion.

In the late twentieth century another technique for induced Abortion was found that utilizes the medication RU 486 (mifepristone), an artificial steroid that is firmly connected with the contraceptive hormone norethnidrone. RU 486 works by impeding the activity of the hormone progesterone, which is expected to help the improvement of a fertilized egg. When ingested not long after conception, RU 486 sets off the monthly cycle and flushes the fertilized egg out of the uterus.
To what level induced abortion ought to be allowed, empowered, or seriously subdued is a social issue that has separated scholars, philosophers, and lawmakers for quite a long time. Abortion was a typical and socially acknowledged technique for family limits in the Greco-Roman world. Albeit Christian scholars early and passionately censured abortion, the utilization of serious sanctions to discourage its training became normal just in the nineteenth century. In the twentieth century such sanctions were changed somehow in different nations, starting with the Soviet Union in 1920, with Scandinavian nations during the 1930s, and with Japan and a few eastern European nations during the 1950s. In certain nations, the inaccessibility of birth control gadgets was a valid reason to acknowledge abortion. In the late twentieth century, China involved Abortion as a feature of its populace control strategy.

In the mid-21st century a few jurisdictions with enormous Roman Catholic populaces, like Portugal and Mexico City, decriminalized Abortion regardless of solid resistance from the congregation, while others, like Nicaragua, expanded limitations on abortion.

An expansive social development for the disposal of limitations on the exhibition of abortion brought about the passing of changed regulations in a few states in the US during the 1960s. The U.S. Supreme Court administered in Roe v. Wade (1973) that unduly prohibitive state guideline of Abortion was unlawful, basically authorizing Abortion under any condition for ladies in the initial three months of pregnancy. A countermovement for the rebuilding of severe command over the conditions under which abortion may be allowed before long jumped up, and the issue became snared in friendly and political struggle.

PRO-LIFE VS PRO-CHOICE

In general, individuals who recognize as pro-choice accept that everybody has the fundamental basic liberty to choose when and whether to have a child. At the point when you say you're pro-choice, you're letting individuals know that you trust it's Acceptable for them to can pick Abortion as an option for an unplanned pregnancy — regardless of whether you wouldn't pick Abortion for yourself.

Individuals who go against Abortion frequently call themselves pro-life. Be that as it may, the main life considered by a lot of them is the existence of the fertilized egg or fetus. They are significantly less worried about the lives of women who have unplanned pregnancies or the well-being of the child after they're conceived.

Rivals of Abortion by and large allude to themselves as pro-life, while advocates for reproductive freedom are normally distinguished as pro-choice. Both groups are of different opinions on abortion. A few pro-life activists might support abortion in instances of assault or incest, while others take a solid position, accepting that all Abortion is murder. Inside the pro-choice development, a few activists battle that no limitations ought to be put on Abortion, while numerous who recognize as pro-choice support regulations that require a holding up period before the procedure can be performed or regulations expecting minors to get consent from their guardian or parents.

CHAPTER TWO

TYPES OF ABORTION

There are two types of Abortion — the Abortion pill and in-clinic abortion. The Abortion pill comprises two unique medications called mifepristone and misoprostol used to end a pregnancy. This medication causes contractions and bleeding to empty your uterus. It's similar to having an exceptionally heavy and crampy period, and the procedure is the same as a miscarriage.

In many states, the Abortion pill can be used as long as 10 weeks after the first day of your last period. Assuming the individual is more than ten weeks, you can in any case get an in-clinic abortion. Your PCP or attendant will give you point-by-point headings about where, when, and how to take the prescriptions. You may likewise get a few antibiotics to forestall disease.

In-clinic Abortion (likewise called a surgical abortion) is an operation, It works by utilizing suction to discharge your uterus. How late you can get an Abortion relies upon the regulations in your state and what specialist or Abortion facility you go to. It's ideal to attempt to have your Abortion at the earliest opportunity because the risk is lower during early pregnancy than after the twelfth week.

In the primary trimester, choices for Abortion normally include:

- Medical abortion
- vacuum aspiration

A woman can generally get access to medical Abortion until around 10 weeks after her last period. It includes taking two types of medicine.

Surgical choices like vacuum aspiration and dilation and evacuation are more normal following 10 weeks.

In the subsequent trimester, a lady might go through:
- Dilation and evacuation
- Labor induction abortion

Abortion is uncommon during the third trimester, however, a specialist might perform it following 29 weeks of pregnancy if a lady's life is at serious risk. They might utilize the very techniques that are utilized during the second trimester.

MEDICAL ABORTION

A medical Abortion requires a lady to take pills at discrete times. Medical Abortions don't need a surgical procedure and are viewed as safe and powerful until the 10th week of pregnancy. The most regularly used drugs for medical Abortions in the US are mifepristone and misoprostol taken together. In such a case, a patient is first asked to take mifepristone, also known as RU-486 or the "Abortion pill," which is endorsed by medical personnel. This medication impedes the body's regular creation of progesterone, a fundamental pregnancy hormone. The patient then requires the subsequent pill, misoprostol, after two days. This medication makes the uterus contract and ousts the undeveloped fertilized egg. Medical abortions are somewhat less successful than surgical Abortions, however, have a more modest risk of contamination.

In early Abortions, as long as 7 weeks of pregnancy, medical Abortion utilizing a mifepristone-misoprostol mix routine is viewed as more compelling than surgical Abortion (vacuum aspiration). Medical Abortion regimens utilize mifepristone, followed 24 to 48 hours by buccal or vaginal misoprostol is 98% effective as long as 9 weeks of pregnancy; from 9 to 10 weeks viability diminishes unassumingly to 94%. Assuming medical Abortion falls flat, surgical Abortion should be utilized to finish the process.

Medical Abortions represent most Abortions before 9 weeks of pregnancy in England, France, Switzerland, the US, and the Nordic nations.

How It Functions

A medical Abortion includes taking two prescriptions that prevent the pregnancy from growing.
This sort of Abortion includes taking two prescriptions, mifepristone and misoprostol.

A specialist or medical attendant will advise about the timing, however, a lady ought to require the second prescription, misoprostol, something like 48 hours in the wake of taking the first, mifepristone.

Mifepristone prevents the pregnancy from growing. Misoprostol triggers the uterus to contract and empty itself, which will start 1-4 hours in the wake of taking the pill. A lady will encounter contractions and bleeding as the uterus purges, which might feel like a very heavy period. A few ladies feel more serious contractions than others. In about 4-5 hours, the pregnancy tissue will probably have passed from the body, yet it can take more time.

Benefits Of A Medical Abortion

- It doesn't include a surgical procedure.
- It is accessible in the first trimester.
- It doesn't need a sedative.

Disadvantages Of A Medical Abortion

- It isn't accessible in the second trimester.
- Just part of the treatment process happens in a clinic.
- It might cause excruciating contractions.
- Sometimes it is not effective

Recuperation from a Medical Abortion

- a few bleeding and spotting that might keep going for quite some time
- an examination with the specialist to monitor recuperation

Risks Involved In Medical Abortion

Some side effects of the drugs include:
- queasiness
- Heavy vaginal bleeding
- Dizziness
- weakness
- gentle fever

CHAPTER THREE

TYPES OF ABORTION: SURGICAL / IN-CLINIC ABORTION

VACUUM ASPIRATION

Vacuum aspiration is a sort of surgical Abortion that includes utilizing delicate suction to end a pregnancy. Specialists normally suggest this during the first trimester.
As long as 15 weeks' development, vacuum aspiration is the most widely recognized surgical procedure for induced abortion. Manual vacuum aspiration (MVA) comprises of eliminating the fetus, placenta, and membrane by suction utilizing a needle, while electric vacuum aspiration (EVA) utilizes an electric siphon.

MVA or EVA can be utilized in early pregnancy when cervical dilation may not be needed.

How It Functions

A specialist starts the vacuum aspiration method by embedding a speculum into the lady's vagina. They then, at that point, apply anesthesia or utilize an infusion to numb the region.

Then, they utilize dainty poles called dilators to open the cervix, then, at that point, embed a tube into the uterus. Then, they utilize either a manual or electric suction gadget to exhaust the uterus.

The Benefits Of Vacuum Aspiration

- It is accessible in the initial 12 weeks of pregnancy.
- It is speedy, with the procedure just requiring 5-10 minutes.
- It is generally torment-free, however, a few ladies experience squeezing, perspiring, queasiness, or a mix.
- It doesn't need an overall sedative.

Disadvantages of vacuum aspiration

- The principal impediment to vacuum aspiration is that it isn't accessible in the subsequent trimester.

Recuperation from vacuum aspiration

- resting for as long as an hour after treatment

- taking antibiotics to forestall contamination
- keeping away from sex for a week after treatment
- Likewise, a few ladies experience cramps for a couple of days following the procedure, and unpredictable bleeding or spotting can happen for a long time.

Risks involved in vacuum aspiration

The likely risks of vacuum aspiration are bleeding and disease infection. In any case, the risk of these difficulties is low.
Address the specialist immediately assuming that indications of bleeding or new side effects happen.

DILATION AND EVACUATION

Dilation and evacuation is a form of surgical Abortion that specialists ordinarily use during the second trimester.
Dilation and evacuation (D&E), utilized following three to about four months, consists of opening the cervix and discharging the uterus utilizing surgical instruments and suction. D&E is performed vaginally and doesn't need a cut. Intact dilation and extraction (D&X) allude to a variation of D&E in some cases utilized following 18 to 20 weeks when the expulsion of an intact fetus helps to improve surgical safety or for different reasons.

How It Functions

A specialist might give a general sedative before doing a dilation and evacuation. This sort of sedative guarantees that an individual feels nothing during the surgical procedure.

The specialist starts by embedding a speculum into the lady's vagina. Then, at that point, they use dilators to open the cervix.

Then, they remove the pregnancy tissue with little forceps. At last, they use suction to eliminate any leftover tissue.

The Benefits Of Dilation And Evacuation

- It is accessible in the subsequent trimester.
- It is a safe and effective method for abortion.

Disadvantages of dilation and evacuation

- It requires an overall sedative.

Recuperation from dilation and evacuation

- Adequate rest is needed.
- May experience slight discomfort and cramping can happen for a couple of days after the system, and there might be some bleeding for as long as about fourteen days.

Possible risks of dilation and evacuation

- contamination
- Bleeding heavily

LABOR INDUCED ABORTION

Labor Induced Abortion is a late-term surgical strategy for performing an abortion in the second or third trimester. In places without the vital clinical expertise for dilation and evacuation, or were liked by professionals, an Abortion can be actuated by first prompting labor and afterward actuating fetal death if needed. This is called "induced miscarriage". This procedure might be performed from 13 weeks of pregnancy to the third trimester.

This kind of Abortion is not common, and a specialist might suggest it on the off chance that a lady's life is in harm's way.

How It Functions

Labor Induced Abortion requires utilizing prescriptions to facilitate labor, which makes the uterus empty over around 12-24 hours. A lady can take these medications by mouth or the specialist might put them into the vagina or infuse them into the uterus. Specialists normally prescribe pain relief medicine or a local sedative, as extreme squeezing happens during this sort of abortion.

Recuperation From Labor-induced Abortion

After the Abortion is finished, a lady will stay in the facility or clinic for a couple of hours to 1-2 days, based on wellbeing and different elements. The specialist can assist with deciding the length of the stay.

Risks Involved In Labor-induced Abortion

The drugs that initiate labor can cause side effects like:

- Vomiting and nausea
- fever
- Frequent stooling

Adverse effects are not common yet can include:

- Hemorrhage
- cervical injury
- contamination
- break of the uterus
- Incomplete release of the pregnancy tissue

Abortion may likewise be carried out surgically by hysterotomy or gravid hysterectomy. Hysterotomy Abortion is a strategy like a cesarean section and is performed under general sedation. It requires a smaller entry point than a cesarean section and can be utilized during later phases of pregnancy. Gravid hysterectomy alludes to the expulsion of the entire uterus while still containing the pregnancy. Hysterotomy and hysterectomy are related to a lot higher rates of maternal mortality than D&E or induction abortion.

Different Old Techniques

In times past, various spices rumored to have abortifacient properties have been utilized in society medication. Among these are tansy, pennyroyal, and black cohosh.

Abortion is once in a while endeavored by causing injury to the abdomen. The level of force, if extreme, can cause serious internal wounds without essentially prevailing with regard to inducing an abortion. In Southeast Asia, there is an old practice of endeavoring Abortion through strong stomach massage.

Detailed strategies for risky, self-incited Abortion includes abuse of misoprostol and the addition of non-surgical instruments like weaving or crotchet needles and garments hangers into the uterus. Such techniques are seldom utilized in nations where careful Abortion is lawful and accessible.

CHAPTER FOUR

HISTORY OF ABORTION RIGHTS

History of Abortion

Abortion procedures date back to 1550 BCE, given the discoveries of practices recorded on reports. Abortion has been a functioning practice since Egyptian medication. Hundreds of years after, Abortion was a subject taken up by woman's rights. The act of Abortion was perhaps the earliest clinical procedure and was performed by unlicensed individuals. The press assumed a vital part in revitalizing help for anti-Abortion regulation. The thoughts of the legalization of Abortion in the late nineteenth century were frequently gone against by women's activists, consiconsideredo be a method for letting men free from responsibility.

Somewhere in the range of 1900 and 1965, there were no anti-abortion laws or rallies since states had proactively passed a regulation forbidding abortion at all levels, including medical and surgical. The only special case for a lady to get an Abortion without going against the law was when an authorized doctor decided the Abortion would safeguard the mother's life. Doctors who give abortions and ladies who have Abortions were continually bugged by the courts and prosecutors. During the 1960s, a few states started to demand changes in Abortion regulation. In 1959, a gathering of specialists set up a model establishment that upheld the progression of Abortion regulations. These specialists recommended that the Abortion regulations ought to give exclusions to ladies that were sexually assaulted or for a child that might have a defect. The Abortion freedom movement turned into a disputable subject in the US in regards to Abortion and reproduction.

US LEGISLATIVE HISTORY OF ABORTION

Abortions were normally done in the US when it was first established and were not confined by regulations until Connecticut passed the first anti-Abortion regulation in 1821. Abortion regulation was passed by state legislatures until the Roe v. Wade administration. By 1967, 49 states and the District of Columbia had ordered Abortion as a lawful offense. That very year, nonetheless, Colorado passed a regulation that permitted ladies to look for voluntary abortion. A few states followed Colorado in changing their Abortion regulations. By 1973, Abortion regulations had been revoked in four states and released in fourteen. In states where Abortions were denied by the law, ladies who wished to end their pregnancies searched out unlawful abortions that were given by medical services workers who are willing to risk their careers were performed by people without the appropriate skills or devices to securely carry out the procedure.

In 1973, the US Supreme ruled in Roe v. Wade that restrictive Abortion regulations were illegal and disregarded a lady's right to privacy. The Court's choice resolved that an unborn baby isn't an individual in the lawful sense. The decision demonstrated that the choice to end a pregnancy during the primary trimester was the sole choice of the lady and her doctor. The choice additionally allowed state legislatures to present guidelines for the subsequent trimester and to disapprove of Abortion after the fetus has reached viability besides in situations where the mother's wellbeing is in danger. The point where viability is accomplished during pregnancy remains a subject of discussion. The vagueness of the term adds to disarray over the legality of state Abortion limitations. Essentially, all state governing bodies don't have the very same definitions for conditions that qualify a pregnancy as endangering the well-being of the mother.

In Doe v. Bolton, a similar case to Roe v. Wade settled around the same time, the Supreme Court reaffirmed its choice in Roe v. Wade by restricting regulations that require admission to a clinic, endorsement by a hospital Abortion board, a second and third clinical assessment, or lawful home in a state before an Abortion can be performed. The choice likewise expanded the meaning of what represented a wellbeing danger to the mother when performing a post-viability Abortion by permitting medical personnel to think about such factors as the lady's age, emotional and mental wellbeing.

The Roe v. Wade choice furnished pro-life activists with a reasonable goal for building a political movement. Activists established the National Right to Life Committee, the country's oldest pro-life association, in 1968 because of states changing their Abortion regulations. Americans United for Life, established in 1971, made a legitimate guard in light of the Supreme Court's decision. Around 20,000 activists walked together in Washington, DC, to fight the one-year commemoration of the Supreme Court's choice in the March for life, which has turned into a yearly custom for pro-life activists. Critics of the court's choice affirm that unborn kids are lawfully viewed as people in different circumstances. Unborn kids have the right to acquire property, for example. Moreover, if an unborn kid is killed, the individual to blame can be accused of murder in certain states. Critics contend that these irregularities uncover the choice's absence of legitimate establishment.

While Roe v. Wade is a national standard for Abortion regulation in the US, the Supreme Court has heard a few cases that challenge its decision. The results of certain cases have brought into question the first decision while further growing Abortion freedoms in others.

During the 1990s, many state assemblies presented regulations that put extra guidelines on Abortion that pro-choice activists contended would bring about the limited access to abortion. A portion of these regulations included that the diagnostic rooms for which the procedure would be performed to be a sure size and width. Different regulations demanded Abortion providers and clinics be subsidiaries of a hospital. Pro-choice groups allude to these regulations as Targeted Regulations for Abortion Providers (TRAP). Rivals of TRAP regulations contend that they put an unjustifiable burden on patients and medical care providers disregarding the Supreme Court's decisions.

In 2015 California passed the Reproductive Freedom, Accountability, Comprehensive Care, and Transparency (Reproductive FACT) Act, which requires Crisis Pregnancy Centers (CPCs) to educate their clients that California offers public programs that give qualifying ladies free or subsidized reproductive medical care, including family planning, prenatal care, and abortion. Clinics should likewise list a phone number that ladies can call to decide their qualifications. Furthermore, the law expects clinics to give proof of their clinical permit or state obviously that the clinic and its staff are unlicensed. The law specifies that this data should be plainly shown at the location and in all print and advanced promotions.

REALITIES ABOUT ABORTION

Condemning Abortion doesn't stop abortion, it simply makes Abortion less safe. Keeping women and young ladies from getting an Abortion doesn't mean they quit requiring one. That is the reason steps taken to boycott or limit abortion never really decrease the number of Abortions, it just encourages individuals to search out an unsafe abortion.

Pretty much every death and injury from unsafe Abortion is avoidable.
Deaths and wounds from unsafe abortion are preventable. However such death is on the increase in nations where access to safe Abortion is restricted or denied altogether, as most women and young ladies who need an Abortion because of an undesirable pregnancy can't legitimately get one.

In nations with such limitations, the law ordinarily considers what are known as restricted exemptions for the regulation condemning abortion. These exemptions may be when pregnancy results from assault or incest, in instances of extreme and lethal fetal disability, or when it endangers the life or wellbeing of the pregnant individual. Just a little level of Abortion is because of these reasons, meaning most women and young ladies living under these regulations may be compelled to look for unsafe abortions and jeopardize their wellbeing and lives.

Condemning or limiting Abortion keeps specialists from giving fundamental care.
Criminalization and limiting regulations on Abortion keep medical care providers from taking care of their business appropriately and from giving the best healthcare choices to their patients, in accordance with great clinical practice and their ethical obligations.

Criminalization of Abortion results in clinical experts not figuring out the limits of the law or may apply the limitations in a smaller manner than expected by the law. This might be a direct result of various reasons, including individual convictions, stigma about abortion, negative generalizations about women and young ladies, or the feeling of dread toward criminal risk.

It likewise hinders women and young ladies from looking for post-Abortion care in cases of complications because of unsafe Abortion or other pregnancy-related complications.

CONCLUSION

ABORTION IS HEALTHCARE

The abortion right movement, likewise known as the pro-choice movement, advocate lawful access to induced Abortion including elective abortion. The Abortion rights movement tries to address and support ladies who wish to end their pregnancy anytime. This movement endeavors to lay out an ideal environment for ladies to pursue the decision to have an Abortion unafraid of lawful as well as friendly backlash. Gaining access to safe Abortion is a general medical problem.

In nations where Abortion is illegal, more Abortions happen without a medically endorsed technique or performed by somebody who doesn't have legitimate preparation or skills. These abortions represent around 4% to 13% of maternal deaths around the world.

Women's reproductive rights are a necessary piece of their general well-being. A huge piece of a lady's adult life includes keeping up with their reproductive well-being, which by implication influences their general wellbeing. This implies access to great reproductive medical services is a fundamental necessity for themselves and the right to safe abortion is only a piece of it.

Abortion is a fundamental piece of medical care. Abortion permits ladies to plan and space their pregnancies, which further develops their physical, mental, and monetary prosperity. Many moms have abortions since it is the best choice for the kids they now have.

For individuals with specific ailments, an accidental pregnancy can be obliterating, if not risky. Furthermore, even with a planned pregnancy, startling misfortunes can emerge. Abortion is a fundamental medical service for them.

Regardless of legislative issues and moral convictions, it is undisputed that Abortion is a medical procedure and is an important part of reproductive medical services. Since Abortion is a part of medical services, it ought to be driven by proof-based guidelines created and upheld by clinical experts — not by political assessment.

Abortion is health care. It is life-saving. When it is required, it should be made available!!!

* 9 7 9 8 8 4 4 4 4 1 2 8 8 *